EXTREME BIOLOGY

Animal Bodies

Extreme Anatomies

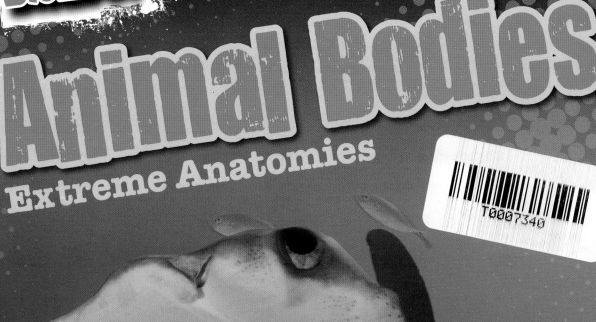

Louise Spilsbury

Gareth Stevens
PUBLISHING

Please visit our website, **www.garethstevens.com**. For a free color catalog of all our high-quality books, call toll free 1-800-542-2595 or fax 1-877-542-2596.

Library of Congress Cataloging-in-Publication Data

Spilsbury, Louise, author.
  Animal bodies : extreme anatomies / Louise Spilsbury.
      pages cm. — (Extreme biology)
  Includes bibliographical references and index.
ISBN 978-1-4824-2231-3 (pbk.)
ISBN 978-1-4824-2233-7 (6 pack)
ISBN 978-1-4824-2230-6 (library binding)
1. Animals—Adaptation—Juvenile literature.
2. Adaptation (Biology)—Juvenile literature. I. Title.
QH546.S647 2015
591.4—dc23

                                    2014027585

First Edition

Published in 2015 by
Gareth Stevens Publishing
111 East 14th Street, Suite 349
New York, NY 10003

© 2015 Gareth Stevens Publishing

Produced by: Calcium, www.calciumcreative.co.uk
Designed by: Paul Myerscough
Edited by: Sarah Eason and John Andrews
Picture research by: Rachel Blount

Photo credits: Cover: Shutterstock: Neil Hardwick; Inside: Dreamstime: Ewan Bellamy 7, Daniel Budiman 45, Terry Evans 17, Isselee 27, Valeriy Kirsanov 4, Thomas Oswald 28, Radub85 5, Stubblefieldphoto 35; Shutterstock: Rostislav Ageev 23, Steve Allen 30, Brandelet 20, Vittorio Bruno 22, Mark Caunt 34, Matt Cornish 26, Jo Crebbin 37, EcoPrint 12, Esdeem 41, J. Allen Frame 40, Neil Hardwick 6, Dan Holm 39, Nataliya Hora 3, 32, Mikhail Kolesnikov 36, D. Kucharski K. Kucharska 15, Ivan Kuzmin 43, Eduard Kyslynskyy 42, Brian Lasenby 9, Lightspring 8, Alberto Loyo 25, Janelle Lugge 29, Matt9122 1, 21, Rene Mayorga 14, Nazzu 33, Yakov Oskanov 44, Enrique Ramos 24, Reptiles4all 10, 11, Mauro Rodrigues 13, Sergei25 31, Beth Swanson 19, Mogens Trolle 38, Vilainecrevette 16, Marty Wakat 18.

Printed in the United States of America
CPSIA compliance information: Batch #CW15GS: For further information contact Gareth Stevens, New York, New York at 1-800-542-2595.

Contents

Chapter 1

Intriguing Insects

Think of the enormous variety of animal species on Earth, from elephants and humans to birds and snakes. Every species has a distinctive anatomy, or the shape and arrangement of body parts. Some animals such as chimpanzees have anatomies that are very familiar or even similar to our own. Others, however, have extreme and even bizarre anatomies.

Amazing Anatomies

Each part of any anatomy has a function that contributes to the survival or success of an animal. Anatomies are the product of millions of years of gradual change in organisms, perfecting what does and does not work. For example, if a bat's wings or teeth failed, it would not be able to catch insects to eat. Parts of an anatomy are interconnected. Our muscles would not work, and we would collapse, if we had no skeletons. Insects do not have skeltons. Instead, they have tough outer casings, called exoskeletons, for support.

Bats use their wings to catch the flying insects that they eat.

Housefly

Most insects are so small that we may miss their extreme features. For example, the common housefly has a spongelike mouth to slurp up its dinner, feet that can smell food, and up to 6,000 eyes! The eyes can each detect light and dark. Bunched together in two large compound eyes, they create an all-around view of the fly's world.

Extreme!

Buzzes and Beats

Houseflies beat their two wings up to 300 times a second. This is what makes their buzzing noise. They also have two tiny dumbbell-shaped stumps that beat in time with the wings. These weights act as stabilizers, so they can fly acrobatically without crashing.

Puss Moth Caterpillar

A green caterpillar rears up at you. It has a puffed-up, orange cartoon face with a big nose and black eyes, and two twirling black tails. You have just met a puss moth caterpillar!

Predator Provocation

The puss moth caterpillar puts on a showy display to make sure predators that spot it and want to eat it run scared. The orange ring and black eyes on its face make the caterpillar look more threatening than it really is, especially when it swings its head violently from side to side. Bright red whips emerge from the caterpillars' tails and wave about. These release a mist of liquid into the air that can sting a predator's eyes.

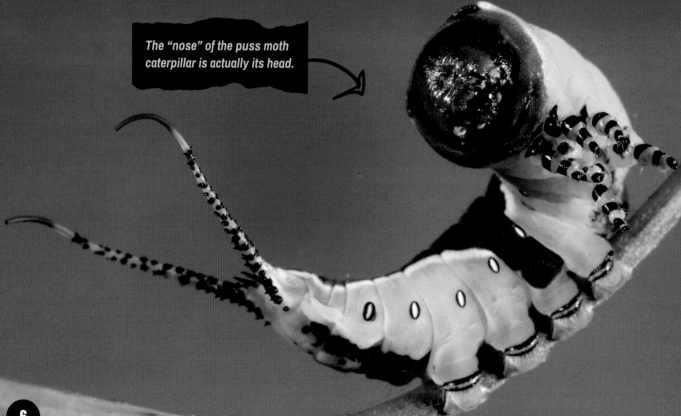

The "nose" of the puss moth caterpillar is actually its head.

This caterpillar is mostly green for camouflage among the green poplar and willow leaves it eats.

Tiny Transformer

The puss moth caterpillar signals it is ready to transform into a moth by turning orange and then purple. Then it spins a tough cocoon of silk and bark around itself. It stays like this over winter and undergoes a remarkable change. Many parts of its body dissolve, and the materials created re-form into a flying adult animal. This is called metamorphosis. The moth that emerges is covered with downy fur a little like that on a cat—which gives the insect its name, puss moth.

Extreme!

Horrid Hairs

Many caterpillars are covered with hairs—but never touch them! The southern flannel moth caterpillar is completely covered with long, fine, tan-colored hairs. They easily stick into skin and break, releasing a chemical that causes itching, burning, rashes, and sickness. This extreme anatomy helps keep predators—and nosy humans—at bay.

Praying Mantis

The mantis may appear to be praying, but it is far from peaceful. Those enormous, spiked front legs are lethal weapons, and the big, googly eyes are always looking out for the insect's next meal.

Awesome Ambush

A mantis stands still with four legs spread out and its head lifted. It moves its head from side to side to track approaching prey. Once that prey is in the strike zone, the mantis's front legs shoot forward in no more than 30 thousandths of a second to plunge spikes into the unlucky creature. The mantis usually eats an animal headfirst with its tough jaws, before flying off in search of the next meal.

A praying mantis has a big appetite. It may eat up to 16 crickets a day. Its front spiked legs fold to grip prey when it is feeding.

Stick insects have superb camouflage. Their bodies mimic the branches where they live.

Extra Extreme

One particularly amazing relative of the praying mantis is a stick insect called a walking stick. It is the longest insect in the world. Its extreme 21-inch (53-cm) body is brown and looks like the branches it lives on. Walking sticks are harmless plant-eating insects and their anatomies are designed to hide them from predators.

Formidable Female

Mantises may strike anything that moves, from insects to frogs, mice, or even birds. That is why males approach the larger females with caution when they want to mate. A hungry female may eat a male, even when it is mating with her! However, all mantises are at risk of being eaten themselves by larger predators such as birds. That is why they are camouflaged in natural colors, such as green, to blend in with the leaves and flowers among which they wait for approaching prey.

Chapter 2
Spooky Spiders and Scorpions

Watch out for these eight-legged hunters! Spiders and scorpions are fearsome predators that have amazing anatomies to help them catch prey. Spiders can live in almost any environment, while scorpions are usually found in dry, hot areas.

To keep predators away, tarantulas release tiny, almost invisible hairs from their legs that sting and irritate any animal that they hit.

Tarantula Terrors

The tarantula is one of the most famous spiders—and no wonder. Close up, these large, hairy creatures look like they belong in a horror movie! Unlike some spiders, tarantulas do not weave webs to catch prey. They hunt at night, using the sensitive hairs all over their bodies and legs to detect the movements and vibrations made by small animals such as grasshoppers, beetles, frogs, toads, and mice. The spiders then follow the vibrations to sneak up on animals in the dark.

Extra Extreme

The goliath bird-eating spider got its name because it is so enormous that it sometimes captures and eats small birds! The fangs it uses to inject venom into its victims are nearly 1 inch (2.5 cm) long. It is also the heaviest tarantula in the world, weighing up to 6 ounces (175 g).

Hundreds of different species of tarantulas live in the tropical jungles and deserts of the world.

Spider Soup

When a tarantula pounces on an unsuspecting victim, the spider bites into it with its large fangs and uses the claws at the end of its legs to grab the prey. The fangs not only hold the prey still but also deliver a deadly dose of venom, a kind of poison. Once the venom is injected, the fangs have done their job and play no part in crunching up the food. Instead, the venom juices turn the prey's insides into a gloppy soup that the hungry spider can slurp down in one meal.

Scorpion

The two most distinctive features about a scorpion's unusual anatomy are huge pincers at the front of its body and a large, curved tail with a stinger at the end. These dangerous weapons make the scorpion a scary opponent.

Powerful Pincers

A scorpion's large front pincers are hard and very strong. It uses them to kill and hold prey and to defend itself. A scorpion either chases prey, such as spiders or insects, or lies in wait until a potential victim passes by. Then it darts forward, grabs the unfortunate animal, and crushes and kills it. If the pincers do not do the job, the scorpion uses them to hold the prey still while it uses its tail to deliver a deadly sting.

A scorpion's four pairs of clawed legs help it run quickly to chase prey or escape from predators.

A Sting in the Tail

The scorpion's tail is made up of different segments, so it can curl forward easily. The stinger at the end of the tail contains a pair of glands that hold poison. The toxic venom a scorpion delivers is powerful enough to kill small animals and even stun large or dangerous prey. It takes a lot of energy to make more venom, so most scorpions use their stingers only when they really have to.

The scorpion's tail is a deadly weapon. It can even kill humans.

Extreme!

Vicious Venom

Some scorpions have stingers that produce two types of venom—one that is lethal and can kill, and one that only stuns prey. The scorpions can produce venom so powerful that it can fend off predators as big as owls and coyotes!

Jumping Spider

Jumping spiders are named for their amazing ability to leap more than 50 times their own body length. However, they also have another striking feature—the rows of big eyes perched on the front of their heads that make them look so weird!

Leaping for Lunch

Jumping spiders sneak up on insects and other invertebrates. Then, when they are fairly close, they propel themselves into the air using their strong back legs, land on their victims, and inject them with venom to finish them off. When these spiders jump up or down, they release lifelines. These are threads of silk that attach them to a surface and stop them from falling if they miss their targets or miscalculate their jumps.

As soon as most jumping spiders catch their prey, they use their fangs to inject venom into the victims.

Having different eyes in rows gives the jumping spider 360° eyesight.

Eye See You!

Most spiders have relatively poor eyesight. However, jumping spiders use their excellent vision to hunt prey during the day. They have two big eyes on the front of their heads and four smaller eyes on top. The two big eyes can see objects clearly up to 12 inches (30 cm) away. The smaller eyes do not see as sharply but help the spiders see farther and judge distances.

Extreme!

Risky Business

To impress a female, a male jumping spider crouches, bobs up and down, dances, and even sings. He sends sounds out through his back legs that vibrate the surface he is standing on so that a female nearby can feel them. All this effort is a risky business, though. If the female is not impressed, she will eat the male!

Chapter 3

Wonders of the Sea

Oceans cover nearly three-quarters of Earth's surface and contain almost half the world's species. Jellyfish, sharks, whales, starfish, and squid are just a few of the enormous range of different animals with amazing anatomies in the world's oceans.

Ocean Anatomies

Many animals that live in oceans have extreme anatomies to help them survive life there. The long, whiplike tail of the deep-sea gulper eel has lights that lure prey near enough for the eel to swallow. Prey animals are rare in the deep ocean, so the eel has a huge mouth, far bigger than its body, which can swallow any size of prey that happens to come near. Jellyfish have remarkable anatomies, from the bell-shaped bodies that help keep them afloat to the trailing tentacles armed with stingers to catch prey.

A jellyfish's tentacles contain stinging cells that stun or paralyze prey.

Leafy Sea Dragon

Some ocean anatomies are all about staying hidden, such as the shell of a mussel that conceals and protects its body. The leafy sea dragon, a kind of sea horse, is a master of disguise, which helps it avoid predators. This strange fish looks exactly like a piece of seaweed, with mottled, leaflike parts that stick out from its body. It uses transparent fins to move incredibly slowly and almost invisibly among seaweeds, sucking in tiny shrimp and fish larvae.

The leafy parts on a leafy sea dragon's body mimic the shape, color, and form of seaweed.

Extra Extreme

Male sea horses can do something that very few other male animals can do—become pregnant. A female lays eggs in a special pouch on a male's stomach. This pouch swells to protect up to 1,000 eggs as they develop. After baby sea horses hatch in the pouch, the male twists and bends to make the pouch split open, so the youngsters can swim away.

Porcupine Pufferfish

The porcupine pufferfish has distinctive looks. On a normal day, it has bulging eyes, a large mouth, a squarish head, and flat spines all over its body. However, when alarmed it can puff up into an amazing spiky ball!

Swell to Survive

The warm tropical waters where porcupine pufferfish live are teeming with many fish on the lookout for meals. Pufferfish can only swim weakly, so they take drastic action to frighten away predators. A pufferfish pumps huge volumes of water, or sometimes air, into its stomach, which is pleated and highly elastic, so it can expand far beyond normal size. This swells its body into a globe, so the fish's outer skin becomes taut and the spines stick out. Many predators are then surprised when their prey suddenly gets bigger and spikier.

Porcupine pufferfish can reach 30 inches (76 cm) long. They eat sea urchins, crabs, and sea snails.

Porcupine pufferfish can expand to three times their normal size in a matter of seconds.

Deadly Defenses

Any fish that does manage to swallow a pufferfish is in for a nasty surprise. The pufferfish has parts inside its body that contain a lethal poison called tetrodotoxin. This poison is about 1,000 times more deadly than cyanide. It paralyzes the animal, which dies within half an hour. The only fish that are unaffected by the poison are some types of sharks.

Extra Extreme

In Japan, some brave people eat pufferfish or fugu, as it is known there. However, they only do this in special restaurants. There, highly trained chefs cut up the fish into pieces to eat without damaging the organs that contain the poison. If one of these organs were nicked, then the meal could become a last supper!

Hammerhead Shark

There is no mistaking the hammerhead shark. This fish has eyes spread wide apart on a flat, wing-shaped head called a cephalofoil. The head looks a little like a hammer, which is how the shark got its name.

Smart Head

The cephalofoil looks cumbersome, but it can help the shark move its head from side to side in the water to catch moving prey. The widely spaced eyes allow the hammerhead to judge water depth and distance better than many other sharks. Sharks can smell blood and other traces of prey very well, but the hammerhead's well-spread nostrils may give it even better sniffing talents. The cephalofoil also has hidden tricks. Sensory pits across the underside can detect electricity made by moving animals, even fish such as stingrays hidden under sand on the seafloor. The cephalofoil locates prey so the shark can strike—like a hammer.

Hammerheads often swim in large schools by day but usually hunt alone at night.

Hitching a Ride

Hammerheads and other sharks often have other creatures hitching a ride. Remora are fish that cling onto sharks using sucker-shaped fins on their backs. These fish save effort by doing this and also feed on scraps of flesh dropped in the water as the sharks feed.

Terrifying Teeth

Hammerheads, like other sharks, have rows of sharp teeth. When front teeth wear down or fall out in the process of catching prey, new teeth are continually ready to take their place. Some small hammerheads, called bonnetheads, have rounded cephalofoils, shaped kind of like the head of a shovel. They also have blunt back teeth that they use to grind through tough crab shells before sucking out the contents.

Hammerhead sharks generally eat octopus, squid, and fish, including stingrays.

Octopus

Imagine your arms growing out of your head—that is what an octopus's anatomy is like! In fact, eight long arms, each lined with two rows of suckers, radiate from just below the octopus's eyes.

Master of Disguise

Octopus skin is packed with thousands of tiny sacs, or pouches, of special cells. These shift around in a split second to give the skin the exact color and pattern of the sand or rocks the octopus is resting on. If a predator is not fooled by this camouflage, the octopus empties the contents of an ink sac from behind its head into the water. Then it escapes under the cover of a purple-black cloud.

Octopuses often drop down on their prey from above and pull the animal into their mouths using the powerful suckers along their arms.

Octopuses can change color with their moods—for example, red when angry or white if frightened.

Shape-Shifter

Octopuses have soft bodies with no skeletons. They use their muscles to change shape, for instance to squeeze into narrow spaces to escape from predators or to find prey. The amazing mimic octopus uses this skill to copy other animals' anatomies to deter predators when it cannot hide. For example, it swims with its arms held stiffly to mimic the fins of the poisonous lionfish and buries itself in the sand and wiggles two arms to look like a sea snake.

Extra Extreme

An octopus has no skull or teeth. Instead it has a sharp, horny beak in its mouth at the center of its tentacles. Its tongue is coated with sharp lumps to grind open shells and scrape out the crabs and clams it likes to eat. Octopus saliva is poisonous and can paralyze prey and even dissolve shells. One bite from a blue-ringed octopus is enough to kill a human.

Chapter 4

Super Snakes and Lizards

Reptiles are scaly vertebrates that lay eggs on land. This class of animals contains four groups with remarkably different anatomies.

Radical Reptiles

Iguanas, geckos, and skinks are all types of lizards, the most common group of reptiles. They usually have four limbs, long bodies, and tails. Crocodiles are huge reptiles with long, toothed jaws and heavily armored skin. The other types of reptiles are very different. Turtles and tortoises have giant bony shells on their backs to protect their bodies. Snakes have long bodies, short tails, and no legs. Some snakes, such as rattlesnakes, kill prey by injecting venom through grooves in their sharp fangs. Others kill without venom.

Crocodiles have 24 teeth for grasping and crushing, not for chewing. They swallow stones that grind food inside their stomachs.

Pythons have camouflaged skin which helps them ambush prey. They can eat animals much bigger than themselves.

Extreme!

Heat Sensors

Pythons have sensory pits along their jaws. These can sense the heat given off by any warm-blooded mammals nearby. This means pythons can locate prey even in the dark.

Deadly Pythons

Pythons are among the longest snakes in the world, growing to lengths of up to 20 feet (6 m). These snakes kill prey, from rats to deer, by coiling their muscular bodies around their victims and squeezing tightly until the prey cannot breathe. They are called constrictors. Once a python's prey is dead and not moving, it uncoils and then flexes and folds its upper jaw wide enough to swallow its meal whole. The snake ripples its muscles to pull the prey slowly into its stomach and digests the food over days or even weeks. Pythons have special tubes leading from their lungs to their mouths that stay open even while the snakes are busy swallowing, so they do not suffocate themselves!

Frilled Lizard

The strange-looking frilled lizard is one of the most extreme animal anatomies in Australia—a country full of amazing animals. It can open a huge frill around its head that is as wide as the lizard is long. This makes the lizard look much bigger and scarier than it really is, surprising and even frightening off potential predators.

Frills and Chills

The lizard's neck frill is a large piece of loose, pleated skin that usually flops around its shoulders like a cape. When the animal is irritated or threatened, it quickly raises and opens the frill so that it looks about four times larger than normal. At the same time, the frilled lizard opens its brightly colored mouth wide and hisses loudly. This intimidating sight scares most predators away.

The frill on the frilled lizard can be up to 12 inches (30 cm) across.

Leggy Lizard

The frilled lizard spends most of its time clinging to trees, where it can scan the ground for insects or small mammals to eat. When it spots a meal, the lizard leaps down to the ground and runs along on its back legs to catch it. Few lizards can run far on two legs because they would topple over. However, the frilled lizard keeps its balance, even when running fast, by pulling its upper body back until its head is over its back legs.

To avoid predators, frilled lizards rarely stay on the ground for more than five minutes at a time.

Extreme!

Out of Sight

The frilled lizard has a smart way to avoid trouble while resting in trees. It plays hide-and-seek. If a larger lizard or other predator approaches, it moves to the opposite side of the tree trunk. If the predator starts to walk around the bottom of the tree, the frilled lizard dodges around the trunk to keep out of sight.

Thorny Devil

The thorny devil sounds like a scary beast, and with a body covered in sharp, thornlike spikes, it looks like one, too. However, this desert lizard is actually quite harmless. It spends its days moving extremely slowly across the sand, searching for black ants to eat.

Desert Defenses

One reason the thorny devil is covered in spikes is to protect it from predators. The patchwork of sandy colors on its back acts as camouflage, so it can blend in with its desert habitat. Thorny devils are also able to keep very, very still in times of danger, which helps keep them hidden from predators. If a predator attacks while the lizard is quietly going about its business, munching up to 5,000 ants in a single meal, those super-sharp spikes stop most animals that try to take a bite.

The largest of the thorny devil's spines project from its snout and over each eye.

Thorny devils may move slowly but they can travel up to 980 feet (300 m) a day across the fiercely hot Australian desert where the lizards live.

Water-Gathering Grooves

The cone-shaped, sharp spikes also stop the thorny devil from getting too thirsty in the dry desert where it lives. Between the spines, there are grooves where droplets of morning dew and water from damp sand collect all over the lizard's body. The shape of the spines allows the water that collects among them to flow along the grooves and into the lizard's mouth.

Extra Extreme

When the thorny devil feels threatened, it takes on a weird disguise. The lizard can tuck its head between its legs to show off a very spiny bump on its back that looks like a false head! This strange knoblike body part confuses predators and gives the thorny devil a chance to get away.

Chapter 5

Incredible Birds

Birds have a set of extreme features unique among vertebrates. They have feathers instead of hair or scales coating their bodies, and beaks for eating.

Flight Anatomy

Many parts of a bird's anatomy help make it light, so it uses less energy to stay airborne. Flight feathers are tough and light, and link together like Velcro, providing a wide surface area for pushing through the air. Most birds have strong flight muscles to operate their wings. Some bird bones are hollow, so they weigh little, and beaks are much lighter than bony jaws and teeth. Birds that soar and glide, such as vultures and albatrosses, have long wings, whereas acrobatic flappers, such as sparrows, have short wings. Some birds, including penguins, have wings but cannot fly. Penguins use their wings to paddle fast underwater, chasing fish.

The albatross has the longest wingspan of any bird—up to 11 feet (3.4 m) across.

Flightless Ostrich

The biggest bird in the world is also flightless. The ostrich lives in hot grasslands and deserts in Africa. It has a small head but big eyes and a neck 3 feet (1 m) long. An ostrich moves around using its long, powerful legs tipped with just two toes. The toes have enormous claws to unearth food and attack any predators that get too close.

Ostriches lay eggs as big as melons. The chicks that hatch are striped, so they are difficult for predators to spot in the grass.

Extreme!

Keeping Cool

Ostriches have fluffy white, black, or brown feathers over their bodies, except on their necks, legs, and under their wings. These areas are bare, so the ostriches can stay cool. When there are no feathers to trap the warmth, heat in blood vessels under the ostriches' skin can escape through evaporation.

Shoebill

The shoebill's beak looks like the front of a boot or clog. The beak is so big that this relative of storks and herons is sometimes called the whalehead!

Brutal Bill

The shoebill's beak or bill measures 9 inches (23 cm) long and 4 inches (10 cm) across. It is thick, tough, and heavy, tipped with a nail-sharp hook. The bird stands still on riverbanks in marshlands waiting for passing fish, frogs, turtles, snakes, or even baby crocodiles. A shoebill attacks fast by darting its head forward, bill open. It flaps its wings to keep its balance as its heavy beak descends. The sharp edges of the brutal bill grip, crush, and pierce the prey. Then the shoebill swallows its meal.

Shoebills have blue-gray feathers and large, yellow-green eyes.

Cooling the Nest

Shoebills nest among grasses at the hottest time of year, when swamplands are driest. They carry bills full of water to pour over the nests. This keeps the eggs cool, so the chicks inside stay alive.

Death Nest

A mother shoebill lays two eggs each year, but only one chick ever survives to become an adult. The chicks hatch with fluffy feathers and cannot fly. They are too weak to catch their own food until they are more than four months old. The parents bring food to feed both chicks at first, but after a while, they feed only the larger, stronger one because they cannot catch enough to feed two youngsters. The smaller chick not only gets weaker but also is pecked continually by the bill of its brother or sister. Soon the unfortunate chick dies.

Adult shoebills are very tall for birds. They can reach heights of up to 5 feet (1.5 m) with wingspans of around 7 feet (2 m).

Sword-Billed Hummingbird

All hummingbirds are small and have bright feathers. They get their name from the humming noise made by their wings flapping as much as 80 times per second. The sword-billed hummingbird has something that no other bird has—a beak almost as long as its body.

Deep Feeder

Sword-billed hummingbird beaks are up to 4 inches (10 cm) long. That is just long enough to reach deep inside the vine flowers they feed on. The bird pokes its beak inside to lap at the sweet nectar made deep in the flower.
At the same time, pollen from the flower rubs onto the bird's feathers. When the hummingbird visits another flower, the pollen may rub off, which allows the flower to make seeds.

The sword-billed hummingbird perches with its head pointing up, so its huge beak does not make it topple over!

Extra Extreme

Every beak in the bird family has a shape related to its use. Eagles, for example, have hooked beaks for ripping flesh, and pelicans have net-shaped bills to scoop up fish. However, some beaks are more extreme than others. The flamingo has a boomerang-shaped beak with special grooves along the edge. A flamingo plunges its whole head into the water, takes a big mouthful, and uses its strong tongue to push the water out past the grooves, which trap tiny shrimp the bird can then eat.

Flamingos use their large, oddly-shaped beaks to separate mud and food from water.

Flight Control

Feeding inside flowers takes precision. Hummingbirds can hover on the spot, fly backward, forward, and even upside-down. Most birds flap their wings up and down, but hummingbirds fly differently, rotating their wings while moving them forward and backward, with the tips making a figure-eight pattern. With this amazing flight technique, hummingbirds can control their direction with the slightest twist of their wings.

Chapter 6
Amazing Mammals

Mammals, including humans, share some distinct features. They have hair or fur on their bodies, are warm-blooded, and feed on their mothers' milk after they are born. The world has an amazing variety of mammals—some with unique anatomies.

The "head finger" parts at the end of an elephant's trunk can pick up things—just like fingers.

Elephant Trunks

Elephants are the largest land animals on Earth. There are two species—African and Asian. The African elephant is larger, with bigger ears and more wrinkled skin. An African elephant's trunk is 6 feet (1.8 m) long and is an amazing piece of anatomy. It is like an elongated upper lip and nose, with two nostrils at the end and pointed parts, sometimes called "head fingers," which are used to grip things. A trunk is flexible and strong enough to wrap around and pull down trees, but the head fingers can do delicate jobs like pick up objects as tiny as coins or crack open nuts.

Elephants can use their tusks to peel off tree bark to eat.

Multipurpose Tusks

Tusks are special long front teeth. Elephants use their tusks to defend themselves, to attack predators, to dig, to lift objects, and to scrape bark off trees. They eat bark in the dry seasons, when there are fewer leaves and fruit around to eat. Elephants also use their tusks to help them dig water holes in dry riverbeds when they are thirsty.

Extra Extreme

The female elephant is pregnant for 22 months—longer than any other land mammal. This length of time in the womb gives a newborn elephant the size and brain power it needs to survive in its habitat. When a baby elephant, called a calf, is born, it can weigh more than 250 pounds (113 kg).

Giraffe

Giraffes are the tallest land animals in the world and one of the most distinctive. No two individual giraffes have exactly the same beautiful patterns of brown patches over their giant bodies.

An Incredible Neck

One of the most amazing things about a giraffe's anatomy is its huge neck. A giraffe's neck is 6 feet (1.8 m) long and very heavy. Despite the length of their necks, giraffes have only seven vertebrae, just like humans, but each of theirs can be about 10 inches (25 cm) long! Giraffes use their long necks to spot danger and to fight, swinging their heads against rivals' bodies. They have very strong bones in their skulls to absorb the impact of these blows, although giraffes can sometimes get knocked out.

When male giraffes fight, they use their long necks as weapons.

A large male giraffe can eat as much as 145 pounds (65 kg) of food a day!

A Terrific Tongue

Giraffes also use their long necks to reach leaves growing at the top of trees and then pull the leaves off with their teeth. However, to get leaves from thorny acacia trees, they have to make use of their impressive tongues, which can be about 20 inches (50 cm) long. Their tongues are prehensile, which means they can curl and wrap around objects and grip them tightly. Giraffes poke their tongues between acacia thorns to grasp and pull off leaves and put them into their mouths.

Extreme!

On the Run

An adult male giraffe's legs are 6 feet (1.8 m) long, which is taller than most adult humans. Giraffes use these long limbs, with hooves as large as dinner plates, to run at speeds of up to 35 miles per hour (56 kph) to escape danger.

Giant Anteater

The giant anteater is a bizarre-looking animal. It has a narrow head, long nose, and a very long, bushy tail. Its legs end in large claws that curl under its feet. These features may look a little weird, but they all help the giant anteater survive.

Eating Ants

As its name suggests, this amazing mammal eats ants, although it eats other insects such as termites, too. A giant anteater has tiny eyes and poor sight, so it finds food by sniffing it out with that long nose. When it finds a nest of insects, the anteater tears into it with its claws to get the animals inside. Its rubbery skin and long hair protect it from the bites of angry ants and termites that swarm out of the nest to defend it.

The thick, bushy hair on an anteater's body also shades it from the harsh sun.

A Sticky End

The anteater flicks its long, sticky tongue in and out of the nest to collect food. An anteater's tongue is 2 feet (60 cm) long, and its mouth makes sticky saliva, or spit, so the prey cannot escape. With that flexible, sticky weapon, a single anteater can scoop up and eat 30,000 ants in one day.

Amazing Armadillos

The armadillo is another strange-looking mammal that sniffs out insects to eat and digs them up with sharp claws. The three-banded armadillo has another neat trick. When it is scared, it can roll into a tight ball, with the armored, bony plates that cover its body providing great protection.

A giant anteater can flick its tongue in and out 150 times every minute!

Bat

Bats are unique in the mammal world. They are the only mammals that have flapping wings and can truly fly.

Winged Mammals

A bat's wings are its most distinctive feature. They are formed from a double layer of skin that is stretched between the sides of the bat's body and the four long fingers on each hand. A bat moves its wing like a hand, which can make it look as if it is swimming through the air. The thumb on each hand is on the front of the wing and has a claw, which the bat uses to climb up trees, handle its food, and fight.

Bat wings have similar bones to our hands and arms. The skin between the finger bones and the body forms the wings.

Fruit bats have large eyes and excellent vision for finding food. Their eyes work well in dim light, just like those of cats.

Echoes in the Air

The other amazing feature bats have is the ability to hunt and find their way around in the dark using echolocation. A bat sends out high, squeaky sounds from its mouth or nose. When the sound hits an object, an echo comes back. The bat can tell what the object is by the sound of its echo. Most bats hunt for insects, and they can even tell the size, shape, and texture of tiny insects from their echoes.

Extra Extreme

Fruit bats do not find food using echolocation. Instead, a fruit bat finds fruit to eat using its eyesight and excellent sense of smell, helped by a set of large nostrils. The bat also has a very long tongue to help it reach fruit and plant nectar. The tongue is so long it stays rolled up inside the bat's body, near its ribs, when not in use!

Chapter 7

Fantastic Features

The extreme anatomies we have seen in this book are all types of physical adaptations. These are built-in features that animals use to survive, whether by getting food, finding mates, or fending off attackers.

Becoming Batty

Amazing adaptations like the bat's wings developed over thousands of years. The ancestors of bats were tiny mammals without wings. They jumped from tree to tree to catch flying insect prey. Those with longer fingers with skin between them could stay in the air longer and use less energy than they would by running and jumping between trees. They and their ancestors caught more food and survived better than those with shorter fingers. Gradually, all bats were born with wings.

The saiga antelope's large nose is flexible and inflatable, so it can breathe clean air during dusty summers and warm air during cold winters.

Designed to Survive

There are millions of fantastic animal adaptations to life in habitats around the world. For example, the saiga antelope's swollen nose has adapted to protect its lungs. In summer, hairs inside filter out dust that could clog up its nose, and in winter the hairs warm the cold air that the antelope breathes in. Birds of paradise have bright, colorful feathers that they use to attract mates in the dim light of the forests they inhabit. Without these extreme anatomies, all these animals would struggle to survive.

Extreme!

Animals in Danger

Today, animals are under threat when they cannot adapt fast enough to the changes humans make to their habitats. There are five main threats caused by humans, together they spell out HIPPO:

H   Habitat destruction
I   Invasive species
P   Pollution
P   Population
O   Overharvesting or overhunting

Can you think of examples of each threat to the animal world?

Glossary

adaptations the changes in or features of an animal that help it stay alive

anatomy body features and shapes

ancestors animals in the past from which a modern animal developed

camouflage a color or pattern that matches the surroundings

cocoon the covering some insects make to protect themselves while they develop

compound eyes eyes made up of many separate lenses or parts

constrictors animals that kill prey by squeezing it to death

digest to break down foods inside the body to get nutrients

echolocation the use of reflected sound signals to locate objects or visualize surroundings

evaporation the change from a liquid into a gas

exoskeleton a skeleton on the outside of an animal's body

fins the animal body parts used for steering and swimming

glands body parts that create vital substances, such as venom or sweat

grasslands areas of flat land with mostly grasses and few trees

habitat the environment in which animals and plants live

insects small animals that have six legs and generally one or two pairs of wings

invertebrates animals without backbones

mate to reproduce or have young

metamorphosis a series of physical changes some animals go through to become adults

nectar the sugary substance found in flowers

organisms living things

paralyze to cause something to be unable to move

pollen a powder made by the male part of a flower

predators animals that catch and eat other animals

prehensile capable of gripping things by wrapping around them

prey an animal that is caught and eaten by other animals

sacs body parts shaped like bags

sensory pits dips on the surface of an animal's body that sense heat or electricity

tentacles long, flexible arms

termites small, pale, soft insects that live in large colonies

toxic poisonous

tropical a region that is very hot because it is close to the equator

venom poison made by animals

vertebrae backbones

vertebrates animals with backbones

warm-blooded describes an animal that has no change in body temperature when its surroundings get colder or hotter

For More Information

Books

Amstutz, Lisa J. *Thorny Devil Lizards and Other Extreme Reptile Adaptations* (Fact Finders). Mankato, MN: Capstone, 2014.

Rake, Jody Sullivan. *Star-Nosed Moles and Other Extreme Mammal Adaptations* (Fact Finders). Mankato, MN: Capstone, 2014.

Waldron, Melanie. *Adaptation* (Essential Life Science). North Mankato, MN: Heinemann InfoSearch, 2013.

Websites

Check out this website to discover amazing animal senses: **faculty.washington.edu/chudler/amaze.html**

Discover some incredible Alaskan animal adaptations at: **www.nps.gov/bela/forkids/alaskan-animal-adaptations.htm**

Read more about adaptation in the natural world at: **education.nationalgeographic.com/education/encyclopedia/ adaptation/?ar_a=1**

Index